I Want to Learn Ayatul Kursi

Written by Umm Bilaal Bint Sabir
Content review: @utrujjah_press
Proofreading Umm AbdurRahmaan S. Bint Ahmed and Assiya Quereshi
Typesetting and design by Umm Bilaal Bint Sabir
Cover Formatting @al.huroof

2023 Al Huroof Publishing
© alhuroof
First Published July 2025

ISBN 978-1-917065-58-0

All rights reserved. No part of this publication may be reproduced stored in a retrieval system or transmitted in any form or by any means electronic, mechanical, photocopying, recording or otherwise without the prior written permission of the author.

All enquiries to: alhuroof@hotmail.com
@al.huroof

All Praise is for Allaah the Lord of the whole of creation and may Allaah extol and grant peace and security to our Prophet Muhammad (sallAllaahu 'alayhi wa sallam), and to his true followers and to his companions (radhiAllaahu 'anhum), all of them.

To Proceed:

How to Use this Book

Learning to read short surahs, or ayaat is a special time for any young Muslim who is beginning their journey of memorising the Qur'aan.

Learning, memorising and understanding the Qur'aan can be difficult all at once. Understanding the meaning can be even more difficult for those who do not know the Arabic language.

This book has been designed as a helping guide for English Speakers who would like to understand the meaning of Ayatul Kursi, as they are learning it. A word by word translation of the meaning* has been given followed by the complete ayah at the end. The explanation (tafseer) of this great ayah has also been included.
*The Qur'aan cannot be translated only the meaning can be translated.

References

The translation has been taken from The Noble Qur'aan, Darussalaam by Dr. Muhammad Hilali and Dr. Muhsin Khan. Tafseer of this ayah has been taken from Shaykh Uthaymeen rahimahullaah and read by Abu Talha Dawood Burbank, AllaahYarhamhu.
https://www.youtube.com/watch?v=4k2mw5Fg100

About Al Huroof

Al Huroof is a small project aimed at producing authentic Islamic teaching aids and material. These are based on the Qur'aan and Sunnah, with the understanding of the Prophet Muhammad (sallAllaahu 'alayhi wa sallam), and his righteous companions - Salaf-us-Saalih - (radhiAllaahu 'anhum). After thanking Allaah, Subhaanahu, we would like to thank all those who have aided in this book, from formatting, checking and feedback.

May Allaah accept it as sadaqa jaariyah from us, ameen.

I want to learn Ayatul Kursi

How do I start?

Let's go over some basic Arabic vowels that you will need for this ayah

Each ayah (verse) has been divided word by word. When you see this little sign it means 'Iqra' (read or recite).

* Tafseer of Ayatul Kursi read by Abu Talha Allaah yarhamhu, as explained by Shyakh Uthaymeen rahimahullah.

Basic Vowels

Dhamma	Kasrah	Fathah

tu bu 'u	ti bi ii	ta ba a

Shaddah

ab-bu   ab-bi   ab-ba

Sukoon

ub   ib   ab

Dhammatayn	Kasrahtayn	Fatahtayn

bunn unn	binn inn	bann ann

Lam – alif

laa

Hamza–alif

'u 'i 'a

Madd

4 or 6 counts

Dagger Alif

This is a long 'a' sound

Hamza–tul Wasl

This sound is not said if connecting with a previous word.

7

Bismillaah

In the name of Allaah

We say Bismillaah before we recite the Quraan. We also say it before we do something so that we can get Allaah's help and blessings in what we do. Saying Bismillaah means we are calling upon all the Names of Allaah.

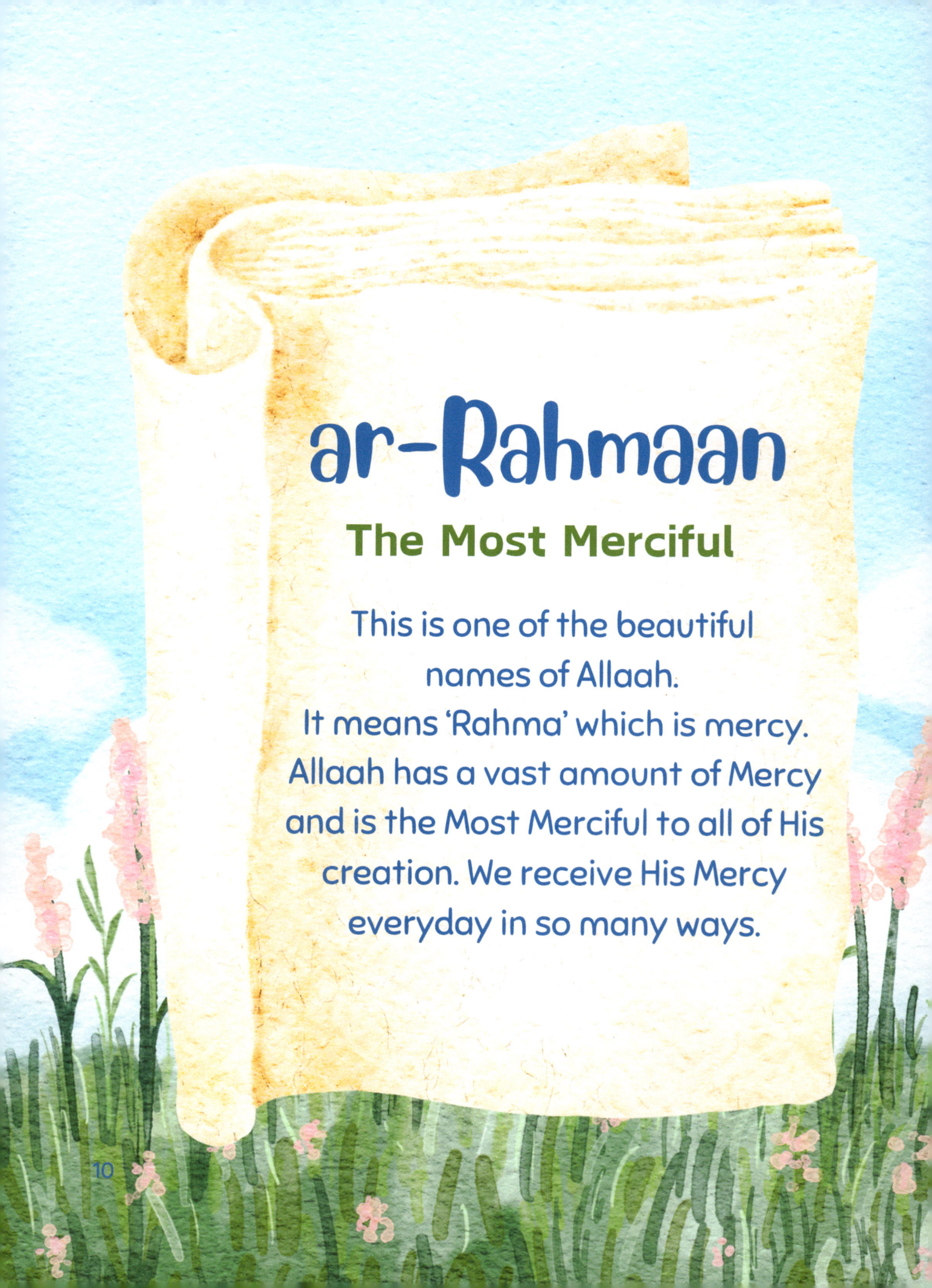

ar-Rahmaan

The Most Merciful

This is one of the beautiful names of Allaah.
It means 'Rahma' which is mercy. Allaah has a vast amount of Mercy and is the Most Merciful to all of His creation. We receive His Mercy everyday in so many ways.

ar-Raheem

The Ever-Merciful

This is another one of the beautiful names of Allaah.

It means He is more Merciful, and gives special Mercy to those who believe in Him, those who follow His Prophets; and His Messengers and are Muslims.

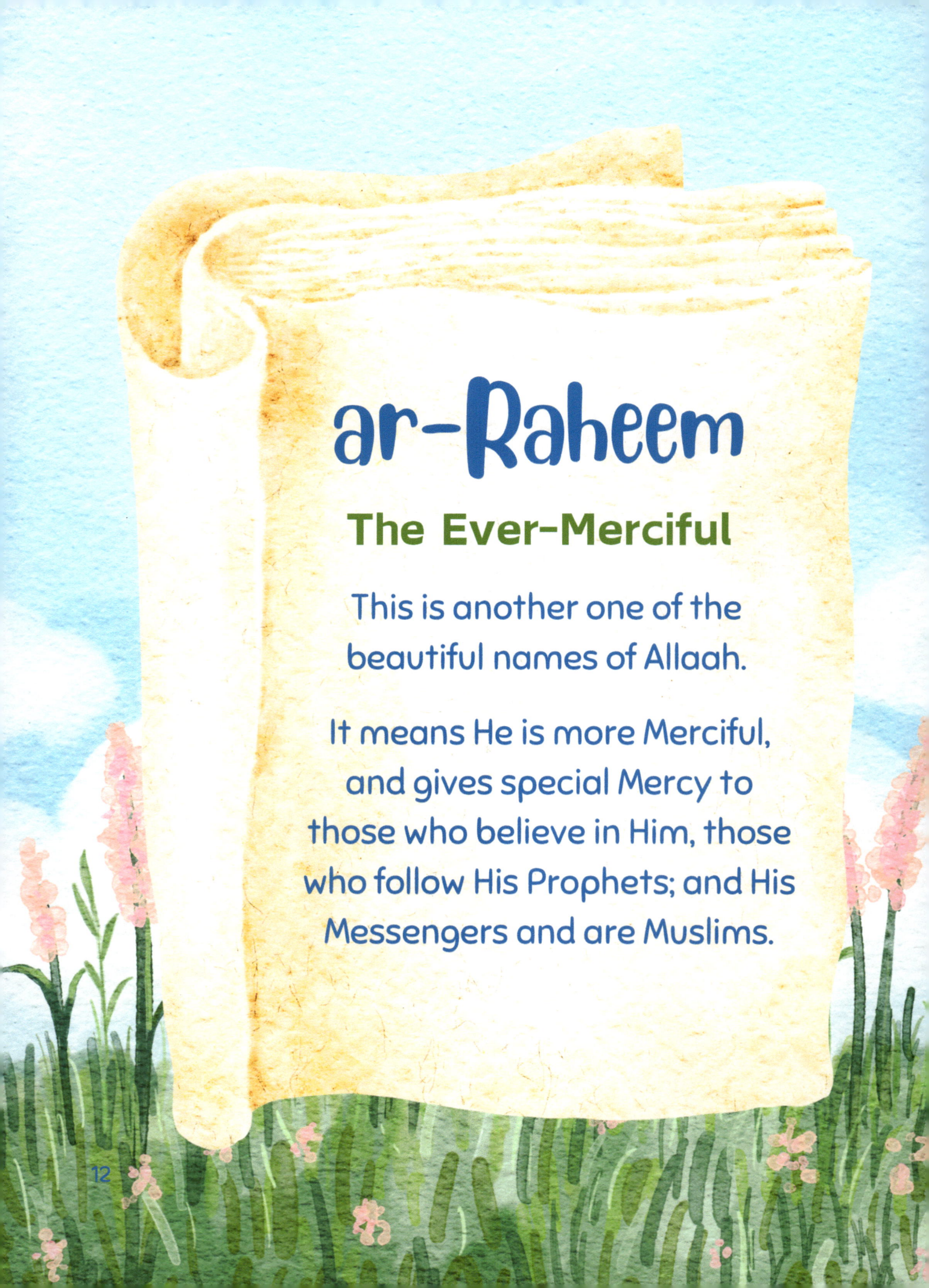

Allaahu laa

Allaah none has

ilaaha illaa

the right to be worshipped except

This includes making Tawheed sincerely for Allaah alone, the Mighty and Majestic Nothing is worshipped rightfully except Him.

All things that are worshipped besides Allaah, are worshipped without right, even if they are called gods. For e.g statues, images, these are all false gods. They are just names people gave to them. They are man made.

Allaah did not send down any proof for them (to be worshipped).

huw-al-Hayyu

He is The Ever Living

Al- Hayy – The Ever-Living the One who is Perfect in His life in every way.
Look at man's hearing and sight. It is not perfect because he cannot hear or see everything. Yet, Allaah is Perfect, in His Hearing, and Seeing and His life is Perfect.

He is the One who is al-Hayy – The Ever Living The One who is Perfect and Complete in His life. His life will not perish, nor will it come to an end.

Everyone on earth will perish but the Majestic and Honourable FACE of your Lord will remain.*

HE is al-Awwal, the FIRST ONE – nothing was before HIM, and HE is al-Aakhir, the LAST ONE – nothing is after HIM.

Surah 55 ar- Rahman, ayaat 26–27

al-Qayyum

The Independent Sustainer of all

He sustains everything perfectly. Al-Qayyum, has two meanings: He is the Self-Sufficient One. He exists by Himself. He does not have any need of anyone.

The second meaning is He sustains everything else. Everything has need of Allaah, the Mighty and Majestic.

Allaah does not need us to worship Him, but we need Him for everything. Allaah says in the Qur'aan: "If you disbelieve then Allaah has no need of you, and He is not pleased with disbelief for His servants, (but) if you give thanks He is pleased with that for you.*

Surah 39, az-Zumar, ayah 7

now say it together

Allaahu laa ilaaha illaa huw-al-Hayyu al-Qayyum

**Allaah none has the right to be worshipped except HE,
The Ever-Living,
The Self-Sufficient
(Independent Sustainer of all)**

laa ta' khudhu hu

He is not overtaken by

sinatu

drowsiness

Drowsiness is something that happens before sleep.

Allaah, the Mighty and Majestic is not overtaken by drowsiness. It can happen to people for example when they are talking, they may feel drowsy. This is natural for people to feel.

wa laa nawm

nor by sleep

Allaah, the Mighty and Majestic is not by taken by sleep.

A person is taken sleep whether he chooses it or not. Sometimes a person may even sleep in prayer!

Our Lord the Mighty and Majestic is not seized by drowsiness or sleep because of the perfection of HIS life. He is the Most Perfect and Most High, and has perfection in sustaining everything else.

Allaah does not sleep and it is not fitting that He should sleep. It is totally impossible that He should sleep, the Mighty and Majestic.

Who could sustain the creation if the Creator were to sleep? No one!

Tafseer of hadeeth in Sahih Muslim Book of Imaan.

وَلَا نَوْمٌ

now say it together

laa ta' khu dhu hu sinna tu- wa laa nawm

He is not overtaken by drowsiness or sleep

lahu maa

To Him belongs whatever

fis-samawati wa

is in the heavens and

maa fil-'ardh

whatever is in the earth

Allaah who is Alone in His Sovereignty of the heavens and the earth.

This includes whatever is in the heavens. and whatever is in the earth. No one has complete sovereignty except Allaah.

Whatever a person owns, like clothing or property, they are never completely free to act however they wish with it. Only Allaah has true Sovereignty over everything.

لَّهُۥ مَا فِى
ٱلسَّمَٰوَٰتِ
وَمَا فِى ٱلْأَرْضِ

اقرأ

now say it together

lahu maa

fis-samawati

wa maa fil-ardh

To Him belongs whatever is in the heavens and whatever is in the earth.

man dhal-ladhi

who is there that

yashfa'u 'indahu

can intercede with Him

This is a question with a denial – who is there that can intercede with Allaah – the answer is no one!

Intercession means to ask on behalf of someone else to bring some benefit or harm. Even great kings in the world can have people who come and ask them without getting permission. Yet no one can intercede with Allaah.

مَن ذَا ٱلَّذِى يَشْفَعُ عِندَهُۥ

illaa bi-ithni

except with His Permission

This means even the most noble people or angels cannot intercede with Him, except with His Permission the Mighty and Majestic. This is because of His Complete Sovereignty and Kingship.

No one is able to speak with Him or intercede with Him – even for something good – except with His Permission.

The most honourable of all mankind, the Prophet (sallAllaahu 'alayhi wa sallam) will not be able to intercede for the believers on the Day of Judgement – except after asking Permission from Allaah.*

Sahih Al Bukhari hadeeth 7510

now say it together

man dhal-ladhi yashfa'u 'indahu illaa bi-ithni

Who is there that can intercede with Him, except with His Permission

ya' lamu maa
He Knows what
bayna 'aydihim
what is in front of them

He Knows what is in front of a person and what is behind them, He Knows what will happen in the future – even if it is by a few moments.

This is because He is Complete and Perfect in His Knowledge.

يَعْلَمُ مَا بَيْنَ أَيْدِيهِمْ

wa maa khalfahum
⬇ ⬇ ⬇ ⬇
and what is behind them

He Knows what happened in the past – even if it is by a few moments.

No one can have such perfect knowledge, because there are many things we do not know. Even when we do know we can forget!

Yet the Knowledge of Allaah is Perfect, When fir'awn asked Musa ('alayhis salaam) about the earlier generations. Musa said: "The knowledge of them is with my Lord in a book. He does not err or forget."*

Surah 20, Taha ayaat 51–52

وَمَا خَلْفَهُمْ

now say it together

ya' lamu maa bayna 'aydi him wa maa khal fa hum

He Knows what is in front of them and what is behind them

wa laa yuheetoona
and they do not encompass
bi-shayy'im-min
anything from
'ilmihi
His Knowledge

The creation can not understand anything from His Knowledge. His Knowledge means anything that is known by Allaah the Mighty and Majestic.

وَلَا يُحِيطُونَ بِشَيْءٍ مِّنْ عِلْمِهِ

اقرأ

illaa bi-maa shaa'

except what He wishes

Except the Knowledge that Allaah wishes the creation to understand. Allaah gives knowledge of the unseen to whoever He wills.

"Allaah is the Knower of the hidden and the unseen. He does not reveal the knowledge of the unseen to anyone – except to a messenger who He is pleased with. Then He places in front of him and behind him an angel who guards it.*

We do not know the knowledge of what Allaah knows – including about Himself and His Names and Attributes, except what He has taught us from the Qur'aan and Sunnah.

So we need knowledge and should ask Allaah the Most High, to teach us what we do not know to help us in our religion and life.

Surah 77, Jinn ayaat 26–27

now say it together

wa laa yuheetoona bi-shayy'im-min 'ilmihi illaa bi-maa shaa'

and they do not encompass anything from His Knowledge except that which He wills

wa si'a kursi yu
and His footstool extends
hus-samawati wal-'ardh
over the heavens and earth

Ibn Abbas radhi'Allaahu'anhu said that the footstool is the place of the Two Feet of Allaah, the Mighty, the Majestic. It is beneath the 'Arsh (Throne), and the Throne is greater than it.*

The Prophet sallAllaahu 'alayhi wa sallam said: The seven heavens compared to the Kursi is like a ring thrown in the desert. The greatness of the 'Arsh, compared to the Kursi, is like the greatness of the desert over the ring.**

The Kursi covers the 7 heavens and 7 earths and the Throne is greater, and our Lord is more Tremendous and far Greater than anything.

**Ibn Hibban as Saheeh, authenticated by Shaykh al-Albani rahimahullaah

wa laa ya'oo duhu
and there is no weariness
hif-thu-huma
in protecting them

Allaah has no difficulty in guarding the 7 heavens and 7 earths. It does not cause Him, the Mighty and Majestic to be incapable of guarding them despite their great size vastness. Even though Allaah is High above, the Mighty and Majestic, He does not miss anything.

Angels guard each person in front of them and behind them by the command of Allaah. Allaah is the best Guardian and The Most Merciful of Those who show Mercy.*

Surah 12, Yusuf ayah 64

wa huwa al-'Aliyyu

and He is The Most High

al-Atheem

the Most Tremendous One

He is the Most High and Tremendous One, High above everything.

This highness is of two kinds: He Himself is High above, the Majestic and Most High, and has the Highness of His Attributes.

He is The Possessor of Tremendousness, and Might, Majesty, Honour and Splendour.

Through these meanings we see this is the most tremendous ayah in the Book of Allaah.

وَهُوَ ٱلْعَلِيُّ ٱلْعَظِيمُ

اقرأ

now say it together

**wa laa ya'oo duhu
hifh-dhu-hu-maa
wa huwa
al-'Aliyyu al-atheem**

and there is no weariness in protecting them, He is the Most High, The Most Great.

When you are ready you can try and recite the ayah together!

أَعُوذُ بِاللهِ مِنَ الشَّيْطَانِ الرَّجِيمِ

بِسْمِ اللهِ الرَّحْمَنِ الرَّحِيْمِ

اللَّهُ لَا إِلَهَ إِلَّا هُوَ الْحَيُّ الْقَيُّومُ ۚ لَا تَأْخُذُهُ سِنَةٌ وَلَا نَوْمٌ ۚ لَهُ مَا فِي السَّمَاوَاتِ وَمَا فِي الْأَرْضِ ۗ مَن ذَا الَّذِي يَشْفَعُ عِندَهُ إِلَّا بِإِذْنِهِ ۚ يَعْلَمُ مَا بَيْنَ أَيْدِيهِمْ وَمَا خَلْفَهُمْ ۖ وَلَا يُحِيطُونَ بِشَيْءٍ مِّنْ عِلْمِهِ إِلَّا بِمَا شَاءَ ۚ وَسِعَ كُرْسِيُّهُ السَّمَاوَاتِ وَالْأَرْضَ ۖ وَلَا يَئُودُهُ حِفْظُهُمَا ۚ وَهُوَ الْعَلِيُّ الْعَظِيمُ

Learning my 1st Short Surahs

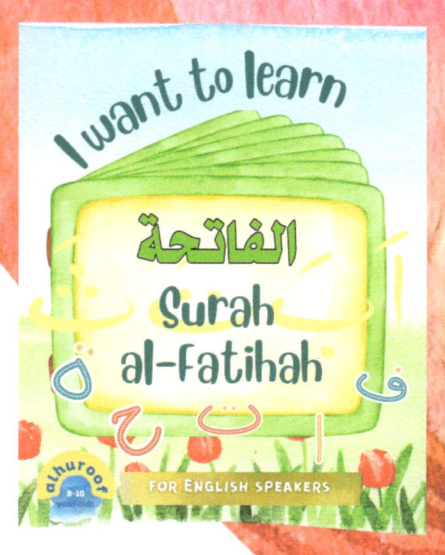  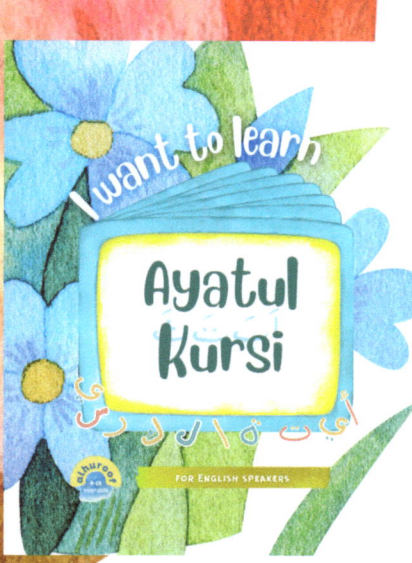

with translation

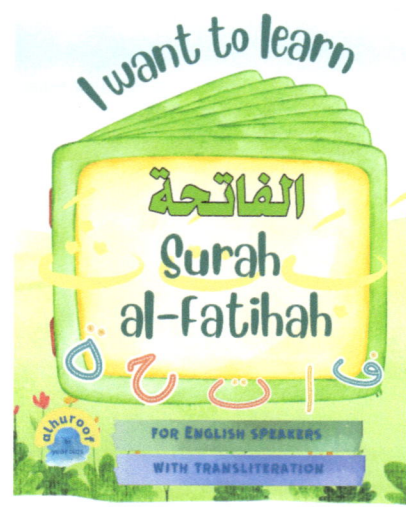  

or with transliteration

 Designed for young or new Muslims

 Arabic and Engish

 With meaning only or meaning and transliteration

 Word by word
Ayah by ayah
Whole surah

Al Huroof Publishing
Little Muslim Readers
الحروف للنشر

ا ب ت ث ج ح
خ د ز ر ز س
ش ص ض ط ظ ع
غ ف ق ك ل م
ن و ه ي

I want to learn
الفاتحة
Surah
al-Fatihah
FOR ENGLISH SPEAKERS
WITH TRANSLITERATION

I want to learn
Surah
al-Ikhlaas
al-Falaq
an-Nas
FOR ENGLISH SPEAKERS
WITH TRANSLITERATION

I want to learn
Ayatul
Kursi
FOR ENGLISH SPEAKERS
WITH TRANSLITERATION

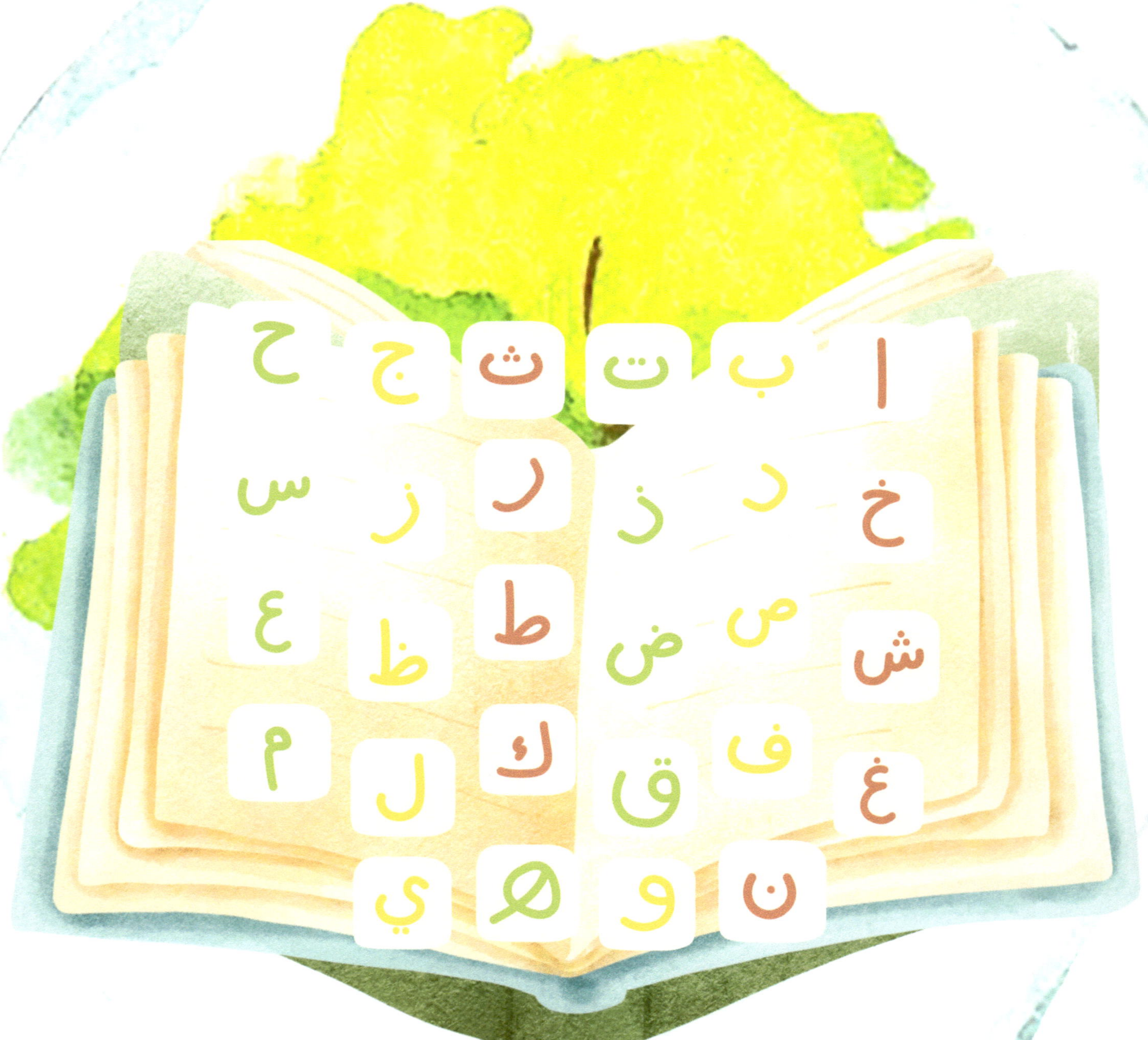

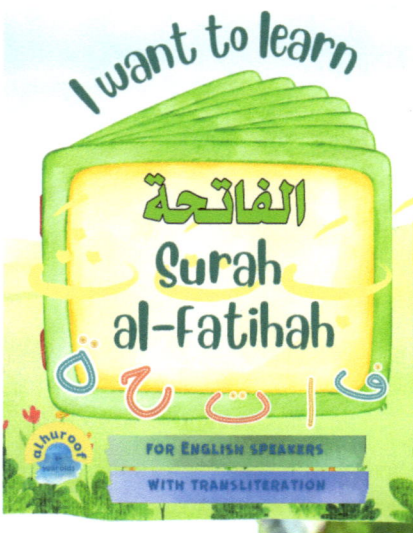

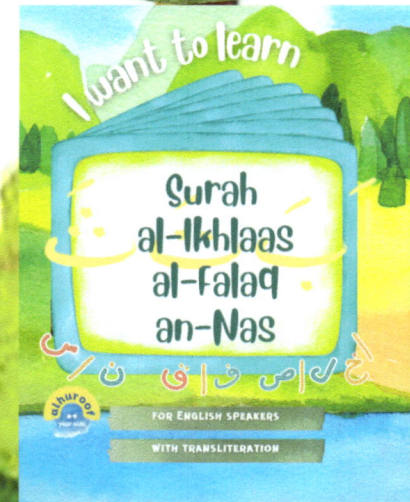

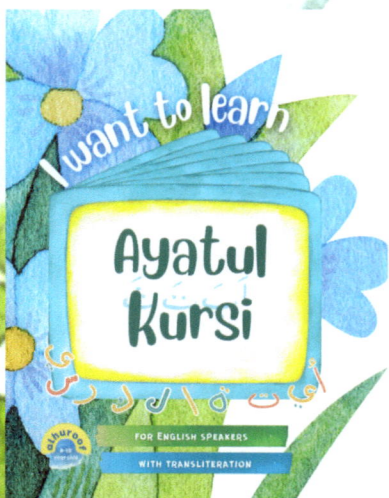

www.ingramcontent.com/pod-product-compliance
Lightning Source LLC
Chambersburg PA
CBHW060820090426
42738CB00002B/50